D1123445

Turnbull, Stephanie,
Mountain biking /
[2016]
33305238553378
ca          06/29/17

# Adventure SPORTS

# Mountain BIKING

## Stephanie Turnbull

A+

**Smart Apple Media**

Published by Smart Apple Media, an imprint of Black Rabbit Books
P.O. Box 3263, Mankato, Minnesota, 56002
www.blackrabbitbooks.com

U.S. publication copyright © 2016 Smart Apple Media.
International copyright reserved in all countries.
No part of this book may be reproduced in any
form without written permission from the publisher.

Printed in the United States of America, at Corporate Graphics
in North Mankato, Minnesota.

Designed and illustrated by Guy Callaby
Edited by Mary-Jane Wilkins

Cataloging-in-Publication Data is available from
the Library of Congress

ISBN 978-1-62588-385-8

Photo acknowledgements
t = top, b = bottom, l = left, r = right, c = center
page 1 Ilya Andriyanov; 2t Andrey Yurlov, b SeDmi; 3 Dudarev
Mikhail; 4 Mel-nik; 5t amadiss, b Glenn R. Specht-grs photo;
6t gorillaimages, b steamroller_blues; 7 Studio37; 8 kuznetcov_
konstantin;  9tr John Kasawa, tl Kletr, cl Florin Stana, cr Sergey
Lavrentev, b Liz Moore15; 10t Diego Servo, clockwise from top
Hellen Sergeyeva/all Shutterstock, Jip Febs, Stockbyte/both
Thinkstock, PinkBlue/Shutterstock; Zoonar RF/Thinkstock;
12 Skylines; 13tr titov dmitriy, l Steffen Foerster, r bogdan
ionescu; Maxim Petrichuk; 15 Catalin Grigoriu; 16 Inc;
17 Pavel L Photo and Video; 18 Raphael Christinat;
19 MarclSchauer; Chatchai Somwat; 21 Maxim
Petrichuk; 22t Siwasan Chiewpimolporn, b J and
S Photography, 23 Oleksandr Chub/all Shutterstock
Cover Maxim Petrichuk/Shutterstock

DAD0063
022015
9 8 7 6 5 4 3 2 1

# CONTENTS

# FEEL THE THRILL

Think you have the skill, strength, and stamina to give mountain biking a go? If you like the idea of muck and mayhem, dizzying drops, and heart-stopping speed, then read on...

## THRILL SEEKER

Eric Barone (France)

**FEAT**
World speed mountain bike record: 135mph (217 km/h)

**WHERE AND WHEN**
Les Arcs, France, 2011

*Mountain biking lets you experience all kinds of wild terrain and stunning views. Get the right bike, train properly, then go on an adventure!*

## Extreme wheels

Imagine the excitement of whizzing down a steep mountain track on just two wheels, twisting and skidding through muddy forest trails, then taking a leap off a sheer rock face. Mountain biking is a seriously extreme sport!

**EXTREME BUT TRUE** The world's highest mountain bike race is in Tibet. The trail goes as high as 18,000 feet (5,500m), where the air is so thin that riders gasp for breath.

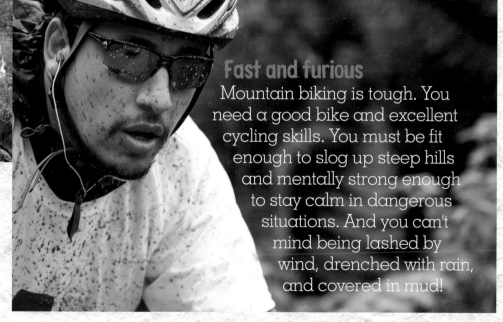

## Fast and furious

Mountain biking is tough. You need a good bike and excellent cycling skills. You must be fit enough to slog up steep hills and mentally strong enough to stay calm in dangerous situations. And you can't mind being lashed by wind, drenched with rain, and covered in mud!

# THE RIGHT BIKE

You won't go far without a good bike. Modern mountain bikes are designed to ride over tough terrain, including crumbling rocks, rough dirt tracks, and fine desert sand.

handlebars

**frame**

saddle

front brake

rear brake

tire

**chain**

spokes

gears

## Bike design

Mountain bikes have strong metal frames to withstand rough rides. They have thick, knobby tires to grip uneven ground, and lots of **gears** to help you cycle up steep slopes. **Shock absorbers** and **suspension** keep the bike stable and protect your wrists and elbows from jolts.

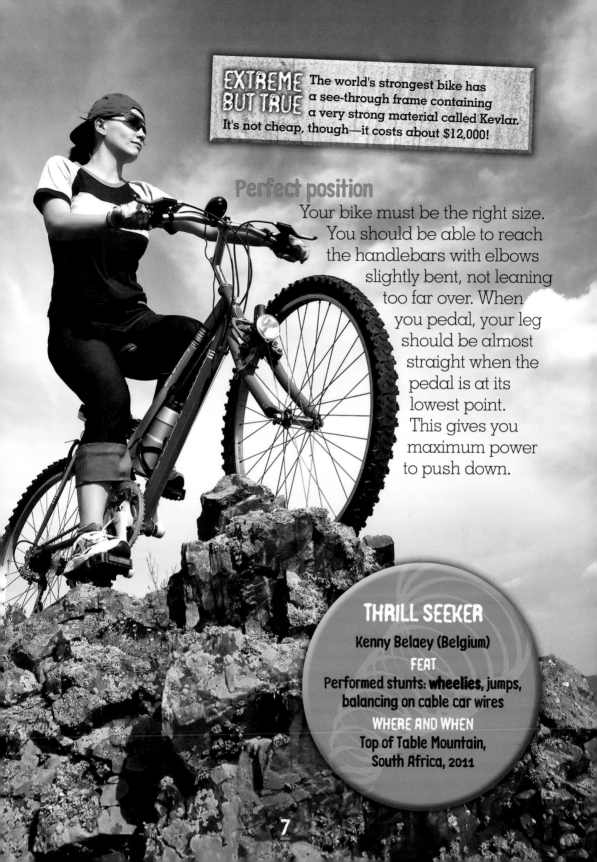

EXTREME BUT TRUE The world's strongest bike has a see-through frame containing a very strong material called Kevlar. It's not cheap, though—it costs about $12,000!

## Perfect position

Your bike must be the right size. You should be able to reach the handlebars with elbows slightly bent, not leaning too far over. When you pedal, your leg should be almost straight when the pedal is at its lowest point. This gives you maximum power to push down.

### THRILL SEEKER

Kenny Belaey (Belgium)

**FEAT**
Performed stunts: **wheelies**, jumps, balancing on cable car wires

**WHERE AND WHEN**
Top of Table Mountain, South Africa, 2011

# GET THE GEAR

Always dress sensibly for mountain biking. Setting out without the right gear could leave you cold, wet, sunburned, sore, or—worse still—seriously injured.

## THRILL SEEKER

Dave Buchanan (Wales)

**FEAT**
48 hour mountain bike distance record: 354.8 miles (571 km)

**WHERE AND WHEN**
Wales, 2011

*Remember that the higher you go, the colder it is, and that weather can change quickly.*

## Protect your head

Never ride without a helmet; it could save your life. Modern helmets are lightweight, with air vents to keep your head cool. Shockproof glasses or face guards are great for protecting eyes from flying mud and grit.

**EXTREME BUT TRUE** Two-thirds of people killed in biking accidents die from head injuries—so you can see how important a good helmet is!

## Dress right

Wear a waterproof jacket and fleece in cold, wet weather and sunscreen on hot days. Padded shorts or pants stop you from getting sore, and gloves and knee pads help prevent cuts and scrapes when you fall.

## Plan ahead

A small backpack of emergency gear could be handy. Pack food, drinks, a cell phone, bike lights, spare clothes, a map, a bike repair kit (see page 10), and perhaps even a lightweight tent.

Mountain bikes may be tough, but they need looking after. Keep your bike clean, check it regularly, oil the chain, and replace worn parts. Don't get stranded in the wilderness with a broken bike!

set of wrenches
(to remove wheel)

## Carry a kit

Be prepared for problems on long rides by carrying a repair kit with these items in it.

tire levers

puncture repair kit

set of **hex keys**
(to adjust saddle)

spare inner tube

## Tire repairs

Punctures are a major hazard. Cut the risk of getting one by keeping tires inflated to the right **pressure**, checking them for stones or glass, and replacing them when worn. If you do get a puncture, follow these steps.

**THRILL SEEKER**

Jason Rennie (Wales)

**FEAT**
Longest jump record:
133.5 feet (40.7 m),
off the top of a ramp

**WHERE AND WHEN**
Wales, 2006

**1** *Remove the wheel, then take off the tire using tire levers.*

**2** *Find the puncture in the inner tube.*

**3** *Use a puncture repair kit to put a rubber patch over the hole, or replace the inner tube.*

**EXTREME BUT TRUE** Some bikers let air out of their tires to provide extra grip. But this makes cycling on smooth roads slow, hard work.

**4** *Put everything back together and pump up the tire.*

# BIKING BASICS

Mountain biking is fast, furious fun, so you must be in control of your bike at all times. Start on easy terrain and build up your skills gradually. Here are some tips.

*Keep a firm grip on the handlebars and pay attention to the track ahead. Slow down if visibility is poor or the ground is slippery.*

## THRILL SEEKER

Bienve Aguado (Spain)

**FEAT**
First mountain bike double **front flip**

**WHERE AND WHEN**
Spain, 2011

## Stay steady

Braking too sharply can make you skid, fall, or even fly over the handlebars. Scan ahead for hazards such as deep puddles, potholes, rocks, and fallen branches, and slow down in time to avoid them. Don't brake while turning corners.

## Get in gear

Gears help you keep pedaling steadily, whatever the terrain. You'll need a low gear for climbing (so that pedaling takes less effort) and a higher gear for going downhill (so you can travel a long way for each turn of the pedal). Experiment to see which gears work best.

*Learn how to adjust your gears by joining a bike club or asking in a repair shop.*

**EXTREME BUT TRUE**

Some cyclists attempt to ride along the narrow, high Yungas Road (or Death Road) in Bolivia, known as the most dangerous road in the world. It takes amazing biking skills and lots of nerve.

## Concentrate!

Always be aware of the land around you and where the trail goes.

Watch out for walkers and other cyclists, and if the going gets tough, push your bike—don't risk having an accident.

# ADVANCED SKILLS

Want to try the steepest, longest, and most hair-raisingly dangerous trails? Make sure you have these expert-level cycling skills first!

## Downhill control

To keep control on a steep downhill run, stand up and keep your weight on your feet, not your hands. Stay relaxed, move backward and forward depending on the bumps, and brake steadily the whole time.

## Safe landings

Going over a drop takes nerve. Bikers dropping just a short way land on their front wheel first, but for steeper drops it's better to land on both tires at once or even the rear tire first.

**EXTREME BUT TRUE** Some skillful riders take part in dirt-jumping challenges, where they make impressive leaps from hills of dirt.

*Good balance is essential if you want to learn stunts.*

## Brilliant balance

Cycling slowly or stopping without putting your feet down is a useful skill. Practice by facing up a gentle slope. Push forward while standing on the pedals and twisting your handlebars to one side. See how long you can balance.

## THRILL SEEKER

Mads Rasmussen (Denmark)

**FEAT**

Long mountain bike wheelie: 1.4 miles (2.3 km)

**WHERE AND WHEN**

Denmark, 2007

# TRICKS AND STUNTS

Some cycling experts use control and balance skills to perform amazing moves. These take lots of practice, but look fantastic!

## Wheelies

Cycling slowly, pull back on the handlebars. Shift your weight to the back of the bike so the front wheel lifts a little off the ground. Don't go too far or you'll flip backward. Now carefully cycle with the front wheel lifted.

*Pick a wide, open space to practice stunts. Concentrate, so you don't lose control.*

**EXTREME BUT TRUE** In one stunt jump, called an X-up, riders fly through the air while turning the handlebars 180° into an "X" shape.

## Back-wheel lifts

To lift your back wheel, push down into the pedals while braking and shift your weight forward over the handlebars. Experts can lift their back wheel high—and hold it still.

## Bunny hops

Combine a front and back wheel lift to do a **bunny hop**. Put a small obstacle in front, such as a piece of wood, then balance keeping the bike still. Lift the front wheel over the obstacle, then the back one. Now try lifting both wheels together to hop over it!

## THRILL SEEKER

**Rick Koekoek (Netherlands)**

FEAT

World record single bunny hop 4.69 feet (1.43 m) high

WHERE AND WHEN

London, 2014

# TRACKS AND TRAILS

Do you want to zoom down mountains, skid around dirt tracks, or try grueling endurance challenges? There are all kinds of trails to try!

## Easy to hard

There are mountain bike trails all over the world. Some are specially made and others are adapted from ski slopes or mountain paths. Some are suitable for anyone, while others are strictly for experts only.

## THRILL SEEKER

Hans Rey (Switzerland)

**FEAT**
Completed one of the world's toughest trails: a cliff path with 4 inch (10 cm) wide ledges

**WHERE AND WHEN**
Cliffs of Moher, Ireland, 2010

## A long slog

Fancy cycling for 70 days? Then try the Great Divide Trail from Banff in Canada through the Rocky Mountains and all the way down the U.S. to the Mexican border. At more than 2,485 miles (4,000 km), it's the longest trail in the world.

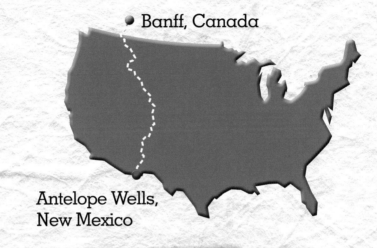

Banff, Canada

Antelope Wells,
New Mexico

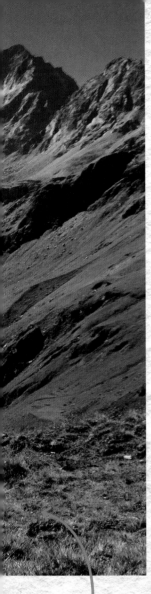

*This fantastic bike trail winds through a mountain range in Switerland.*

EXTREME
BUT TRUE

The famous Slickrock Trail twists and turns for 10.5 miles (17 km) in Utah, almost entirely over bright orange sandstone.

## Find out more

Join a mountain biking club, which will take you on trails in your area, or ask at a local bike shop. Pay attention to warnings—if they say it's for advanced riders only, they mean it!

# DAREDEVIL RACING

Mountain bike experts compete in speed races, off-road races, jumping events, and stunt challenges. They're dangerous but exciting to watch!

Cyclists often skid and fall as they hurtle down slopes, like these racers in Thailand.

## THRILL SEEKER
Sam Hill (Australia)
FEAT
Mountain Bike World Champion
WHERE AND WHEN
Monte Sainte-Anne, Canada
2010

## Let's race

Important riding competitions include the Mountain Bike World Championship and World Cup. Since 1996, mountain biking has also been an **Olympic** sport. Start by getting involved in local races and work your way up!

*Riders tackle treacherous snow-covered rocks in this cross-country race in Kazakhstan.*

## Race types

Some races are downhill sprints to the finish line; others are endurance events across difficult terrain, often in snow and ice. Bike marathons are 50-mile (80-km) trails across mountains, and **free ride** events combine racing with skills such as stunt moves.

**EXTREME BUT TRUE** Missy Giove (nicknamed "The Missile") is a former championship mountain bike racer. During her impressive career she broke her hand, kneecap, heel, wrist, pelvis, collar bone, and teeth!

# GLOSSARY

**bunny hop**
A jump straight up in the air with both wheels off the ground, landing on both wheels. Bunny hops are often used in stunts, but they're also a great way of springing over obstacles while riding.

**chain**
Lots of linked metal rollers that connect the pedals with the back wheel. As you push the pedals, the chain turns the back wheel and the bike moves forward.

**frame**
The main structure of a bike, made of metal tubes.

**free ride**
Riding that focuses on tricks and technical ability. It includes obstacles such as ramps to jump from, and narrow planks to balance on. Riders try to cover the course at speed and with style.

**front flip**
A bike stunt involving turning over in the air, head first, then landing safely on both wheels. Riders zoom off a steep ramp to attempt this.

**gear**
A device that controls how fast a bike wheel turns in relation to how fast you pedal. Mountain bikes have several gears.

hex keys

**hex key**
An L-shaped tool with six sides used to tighten or loosen six-sided screws. Hex keys come in several sizes.

**Olympic**
Part of the Olympic Games, held every four years. Cross-country mountain biking has been an Olympic event since 1996.

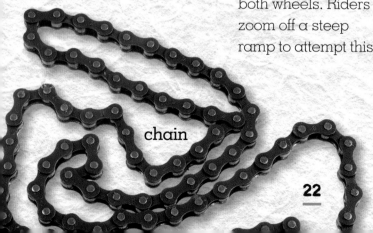

chain

**pressure**
The amount of air in a tire. Air gradually escapes as you ride, so remember to check tires regularly and use a pump to top them up to the correct pressure (measured in units called psi).

**shock absorber**
A mechanical device that absorbs, or soaks up, energy from the movement of the bike's wheels as they jolt over rough ground. Shock absorbers work with the bike's suspension system to make riding smoother and more comfortable.

**suspension**
A system of springs that cushions a mountain bike from bumps and jolts as it goes over uneven ground.

**wheelie**
A way of cycling along with the front wheel lifted off the ground.

pump

WEBSITES

**www.imba.com**
Read news and information from the International Mountain Bike Association.

**www.bicycling.com/mountain-bike**
Find out what's going on in the world of mountain biking and read advice on how to look after your bike.

**bikemagic.com/mountain-bike-trails/cycle-routes/ top-5-worldwide-mountain-bike-destinations.html**
Take a look at some of the world's top mountain bike trails.

# INDEX